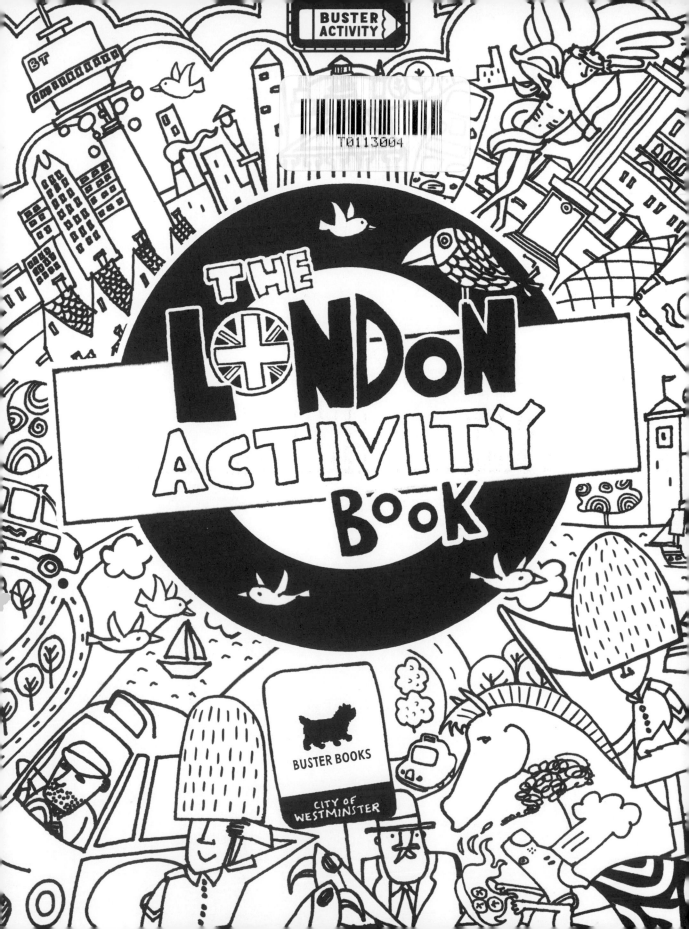

BUSTER ACTIVITY

T0113004

THE LONDON ACTIVITY BOOK

BUSTER BOOKS

CITY OF WESTMINSTER

Written by Ellen Bailey
Illustrated by Andrew Pinder and Julian Mosedale
Edited by Sophie Schrey

Cover design by Angie Allison
Designed by Barbara Ward

First published in Great Britain in 2013 by Buster Books,
an imprint of Michael O'Mara Books Limited,
9 Lion Yard, Tremadoc Road, London SW4 7NQ

This revised edition was first published in 2024 by Buster Books.

W www.mombooks.com/buster
f Buster Books
𝕏 @BusterBooks
⊙ @buster_books

Copyright © Buster Books 2012, 2013, 2024

This book contains some images taken from *The London Colouring Book* previously published by Buster Books.

All rights reserved. No part of this publication may be reproduced, stored in a retrieval system, or transmitted by any means, without the prior permission in writing of the publisher, nor be otherwise circulated in any form of binding or cover other than that in which it is published and without a similar condition including this condition being imposed on the subsequent purchaser.

A CIP catalogue record for this book is available from the British Library.

ISBN: 978-1-78055-979-7

1 3 5 7 9 10 8 6 4 2

This book was printed in November 2023 by Leo Paper Products Ltd, Heshan Astros Printing Limited, Xuantan Temple Industrial Zone, Gulao Town, Heshan City, Guangdong Province, China.

The publisher and author disclaim, as far as is legally permissible, all liability for accidents, or injuries, or loss that may occur as a result of information or instructions given in this book. Use your best common sense at all times – always wear appropriate safety gear, be very careful with scissors and when using the oven, stay within the law and local rules, and be considerate of other people.

CONTENTS

WELCOME TO LONDON!

Get ready for an exciting tour of this amazing city. There are lots of things for you to do along the way, from puzzle challenges and games to play, to fun things to make and cool pictures to colour and complete.

Your first stop is to colour in the famous London scenes on this page … so what are you waiting for?

THE TOWER OF LONDON

William the Conqueror began building the Tower of London in the late 1070s. Over the centuries, the Tower has witnessed many important events in British history.

The Tower of London sits on the banks of the River Thames and is one of the biggest and most important castles in England.

Over the years it has been home to many kings and queens, who used it for tournaments, coronation celebrations (the ceremony where a ruler is crowned) and victory parties. But the Tower has a darker side … it has been used as a prison, and a place of torture, murder and execution.

MOAT GETAWAY

The Tower was protected by a deep moat, filled with water. Can you help this prisoner escape across it? He has stolen a large bag of jewels, and has promised to give half of these to the Yeoman Warder (a guard, also known as a 'Beefeater') if he helps him escape. During his time in prison, he has also made friends with a lion who he wants to set free.

The prisoner has a rowboat that can only carry him and one other thing. The lion hates the Yeoman Warder, and if they are left alone together the lion will eat him. If the Yeoman Warder is left alone with the jewels, he will steal them. Can you find a way to get them all safely across to the other side of the moat?

You'll find the solution on page 63.

Yeoman Warder

Prisoner

Lion

Jewels

THE ROYAL MENAGERIE

England's kings and queens kept a variety of wild animals at the Tower, in a place called the Royal Menagerie.

Can you guess from the descriptions below what each animal got up to? Check your answers on page 63.

- This mighty beast roared from its own specially built tower in the grounds

- This cheeky creature drank ale from the soldiers' canteen

- This animal tore up visitors' umbrellas

- This feathery creature was fed nails as people believed it could digest metal

- This animal used to fish in the River Thames

ARRANGE THE ARMOURY

A king's armour protected him in battle and during tournaments. Can you complete the grid so that each row, each column and each outlined block of four squares contains only one **H**elmet, one **C**uirass (special armour designed to cover the chest), one **P**istol, and one **S**haffron (the armour used to protect a horse's head during battle)? The answer is on page 63. Let the battle begin!

DID YOU KNOW?

Legend has it that the kingdom will fall if there are ever less than six ravens in the Tower. How many ravens can you spot across these two pages?

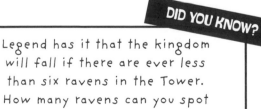
H   C   P   S

FEARSOME FAMILIES

Ever wished you could lock your brother or sister in a tower? Well, for some of the prisoners at the Tower of London, it was members of their own family that were holding them captive!

UNBELIEVABLE UNCLE

In 1483, the sons of King Edward IV, 12-year-old Edward and his younger brother Richard, were imprisoned in the Tower. They were never seen again. This left the way clear for their uncle to become king, so it seems likely that the brothers were murdered. In 1674, two boy-sized skeletons were found when a building at the Tower was demolished.

SUSPICIOUS SISTER

Before Elizabeth I became queen she was imprisoned in the Tower by her sister Mary. She was accused of plotting to seize the throne, but there was so little evidence against her that she was released. Elizabeth hated the Tower because it was the place where her mother, Anne Boleyn, had been executed, but in 1559 she returned there to celebrate her own coronation.

CRUEL COUSIN

On 10th July 1553, 16-year-old Lady Jane Grey was declared Queen of England. She ruled for only nine days before her cousin Mary, who wanted the throne herself, had Jane arrested. She was charged with high treason (a crime against your country) and sentenced to death. She was beheaded at the Tower with a single blow of the axe.

COLOUR IN THE SERPENTINE IN HYDE PARK.

SAVE THE CROWN JEWELS!

The Crown Jewels are housed in the Tower of London. The person who came closest to stealing the royal treasures was Colonel Blood in 1671. Can you chase the thieves through the Tower and return the jewels to King Charles II?

Start at the Jewel House where the keeper has been tied up. You must pass Colonel Blood, who is trying to hide a crown under his cloak, Blood's son, who is trying to saw a sceptre in half, and their friend, Robert Perot, who has stuck an orb down his trousers!

The Yeoman Warders might mistake you for a thief and arrest you, so make sure you don't pass any on your route. If your path is blocked by a raven or an animal, you cannot pass – and they might attack you, so beware! The solution is on page 64. Good luck!

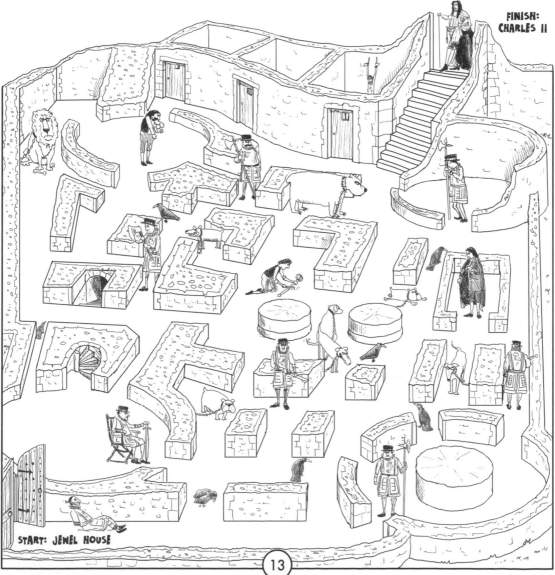

FINISH: CHARLES II

START: JEWEL HOUSE

COLOUR IN HENRY VIII AT HAMPTON COURT PALACE.

THE GRUESOME AILMENTS OF HENRY VIII

When Henry VIII was a young man, he was very good looking. He was famous for having a strong, powerful body. As he got older, however, his health deteriorated and he was afflicted with all sorts of gruesome and disgusting illnesses.

Can you match these ancient remedies to each of Henry's ailments?
One has been done to get you started. The answers are on page **64**.

1. Headaches that made him very moody.

A. A paste made from worms, bone marrow from pigs and a red-haired dog that has been boiled in oil. This was meant to reduce swelling.

2. Digestion problems from eating rich food.

B. Rosemary was used in cooking to help digest food.

3. Gout - painful swollen joints.

C. Strong-smelling perfumes disguised bad pongs.

4. Bags under his eyes from lack of sleep.

D. Rubbing his forehead with a rope that had been used to hang a criminal.

5. Pongy ulcers that oozed pus.

E. Lavender to help him sleep.

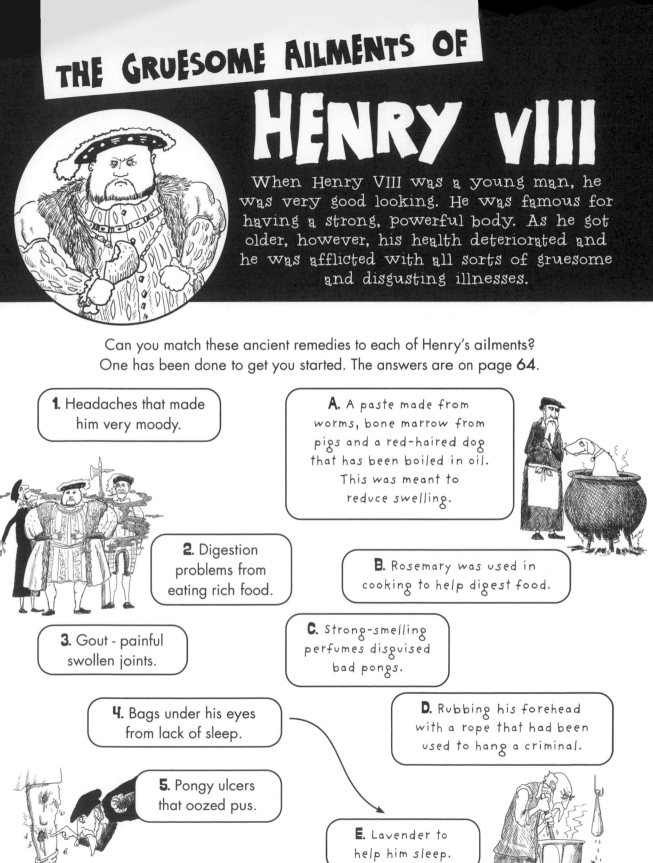

SIX WIVES' OLYMPICS

Henry VIII is famous for having six wives.

Create your own Six Wives' Olympics course by setting up the stations below. Time yourself to see how quickly you can complete it.

STATION 1: KATHERINE OF ARAGON

Katherine was a young princess from Aragon, Spain who was married to Henry for almost 24 years before they were divorced.

SET UP: Find two pieces of A4 paper. Draw the Aragon flag on one piece, and the English flag on the other and colour them in. Use the pictures opposite for guidance. Place one flag on the floor. Take a large step to the right and place the other flag on the floor.

CHALLENGE: Stand in front of the Aragon flag and jump sideways so that you're in front of the English flag, then jump back in front of the Spanish flag. Repeat 24 times.

Aragon flag   English flag

Yellow   Red   White   Red

STATION 2: ANNE BOLEYN

Anne was married to the King for just three years before she was beheaded.

SET UP: Find a piece of paper and a tennis ball. Screw up the paper and use a thick marker pen to draw a face on the front, to create Anne Boleyn's head. Place the head on the ground and take three big steps back.

CHALLENGE: Kneel on the ground and roll the tennis ball towards the head. The aim is to hit the paper ball, beheading Anne.

STATION 3: JANE SEYMOUR

Jane gave Henry the male heir he had been waiting for (Edward VI) but she died soon afterwards. The Queen never had a proper coronation because at that time the plague was raging in London.

SET UP: You will need a piece of newspaper, some sticky tape and scissors.

CHALLENGE: Make a paper crown for Jane as quickly as you can! It needs to look like a crown and stay on your head without you holding it.

STATION 4: ANNE OF CLEVES

Henry married Anne after seeing a painting of her. When he saw her in the flesh, however, Henry found her rather unattractive and divorced her.

SET UP: Find a piece of paper, some colouring pencils, and some sticky tack or masking tape.

CHALLENGE: Draw a picture of Anne as quickly as you can and stick it up on the wall.

STATION 5: CATHERINE HOWARD

Catherine was just a teenager when she married Henry. She was only married to the King for 18 months before she was beheaded.

SET UP: Return to Station 2. Use a new piece of paper to create a paper head for Catherine. Place the head on the ground and take five big steps back.

CHALLENGE: Kneel on the ground and roll the tennis ball towards the head, until you have beheaded Catherine.

DID YOU KNOW?
The rhyme 'divorced, beheaded, died, divorced, beheaded, survived' describes how each one of Henry's wives met their end.

STATION 6: KATHERINE PARR

Katherine was married to Henry until he died in 1547, so she survived!

SET UP: To complete this station you need a skipping rope.

CHALLENGE: Skip until you have repeated the rhyme 'Divorced, beheaded, died, divorced, beheaded, survived' six times.

How quickly did you complete the course? Write your time in here.

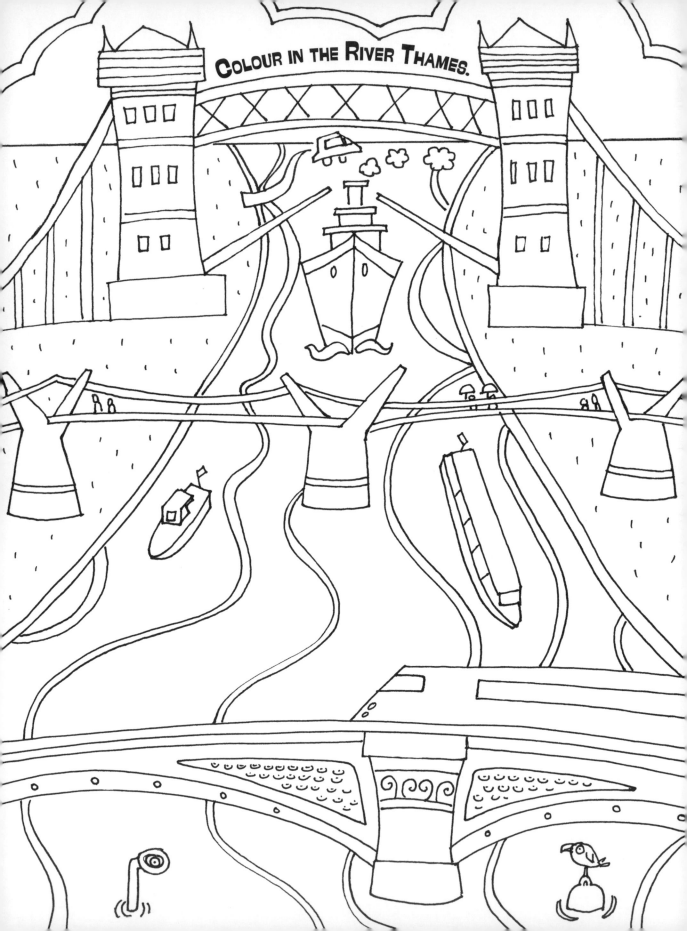

COLOUR IN THE RIVER THAMES.

THE GREAT STINK

During Tudor times, some courtiers used a special toilet known as the 'common jakes' that could fit 28 people at a time! The toilet drained into the River Thames. As most other Londoners also emptied their waste into the river, the Thames was essentially one giant sewer. The smell was revolting!

Doodle stinky things to make the river really pong.

Design a coat of arms ...

DID YOU KNOW?
Jousting was a sport played by noblemen during medieval times. It was one of King Henry VIII's favourite pastimes and during one tournament, a lance (a long spear-like weapon) nearly took his head clean off!

... and decorate the horse.

AMAZING MAZE

King William III has lost one of his green stockings in the maze at Hampton Court and is offering a reward to the person who returns it to him in the middle of the maze.

Hampton Court Palace

Can you find your way through the maze to collect the stocking and return it to the King? The solution is on page **64**.

King William III → FINISH

START

COLOUR IN THE LORD MAYOR'S SHOW.

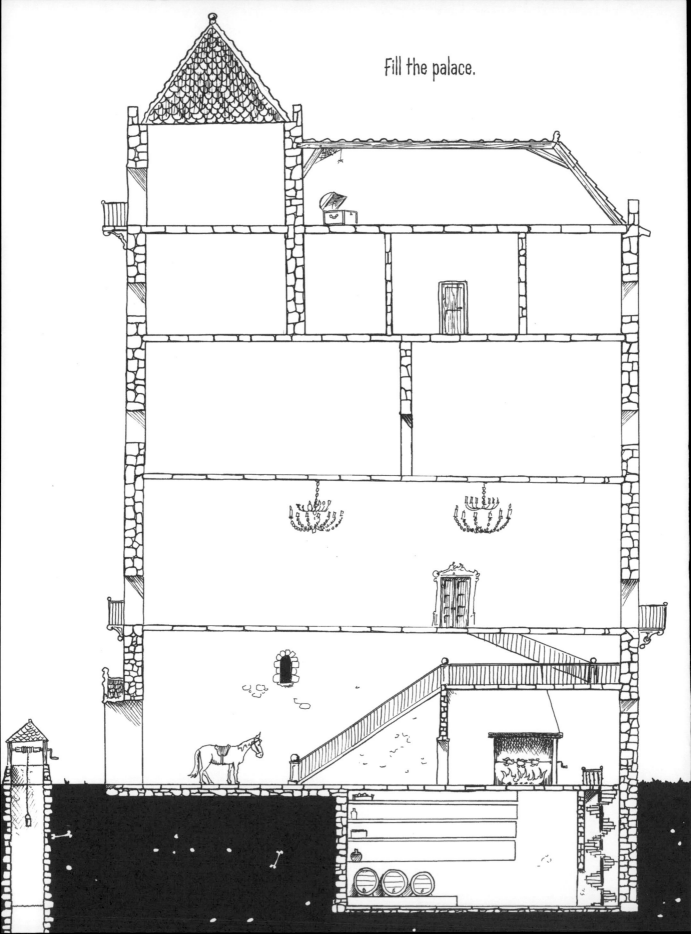

Fill the palace.

THE CARDINAL SPIDER WEB

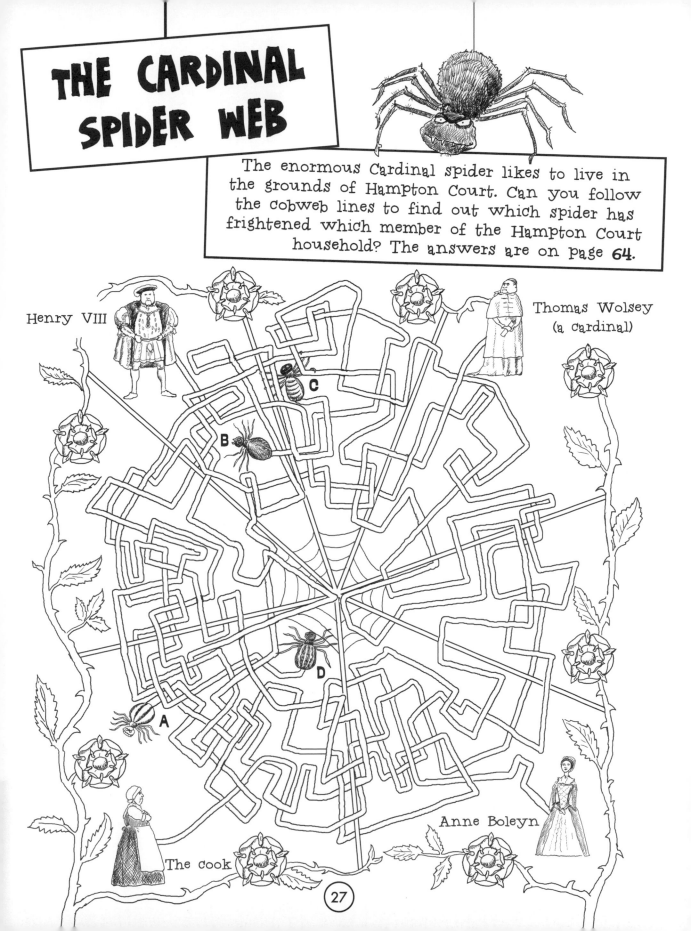

The enormous Cardinal spider likes to live in the grounds of Hampton Court. Can you follow the cobweb lines to find out which spider has frightened which member of the Hampton Court household? The answers are on page 64.

Henry VIII

Thomas Wolsey
(a cardinal)

C

B

D

A

The cook

Anne Boleyn

COLOUR IN THE STATUE
OF PETER PAN IN
KENSINGTON GARDENS.

MAKE YOUR OWN TUDOR KNOT GARDEN

During his time at Hampton Court, Henry VIII created legendary gardens with plants arranged in 'knot' patterns. Follow these simple steps to create your very own Tudor knot garden.

YOU WILL NEED:

- A thick black pen
- A large sponge cloth
- Scissors
- Cress seeds
- Water
- A tray

1. Use a thick black pen to draw a knot design on to the sponge cloth.

You could copy one of the examples below, or design your own.

2. Carefully cut out your design.

3. Soak the sponge cloth in water, then place it in the tray.

4. Sprinkle cress seeds all over the sponge cloth.

5. Place the tray on a windowsill and water frequently and watch your Tudor knot garden grow!

COLOUR IN THIS ROYAL SCENE.

NELSON'S BODY PARTS

Admiral Horatio Lord Nelson left home and joined the navy when he was just 12 years old. He is famous for his victories in battles against the French. During these battles he lost the sight in his right eye and lost his right arm.

Play this gruesome game with a friend and seriously gross them out!

Nelson's hat

YOU WILL NEED:

A blindfold (a large handkerchief works well)

ITEM 1: A hat (ideally one like Nelson would have worn!)

ITEM 2: A coat made of wool or cloth

ITEM 3: A metal badge (Nelson's medal)

ITEM 4: A rolling pin (Nelson's wooden arm)

MYSTERY ITEM: A grape with the skin removed (Nelson's missing eye).

Nelson's medal

1. Blindfold your friend, keeping the items hidden from view until you are sure they cannot see anything.

2. Hand your friend each of the four items in turn, and explain to them which part of Nelson they are holding.

3. Once they have felt each item, tell them there is now a Mystery Item that is another one of Nelson's missing body parts … then hand them the peeled grape.

Cover your ears as they scream in disgust when you say, '… and this is Nelson's missing eye!'

COLOUR IN NELSON'S COLUMN AT TRAFALGAR SQUARE.

COLOUR IN THE TRAFFIC JAM AT PICCADILLY CIRCUS.

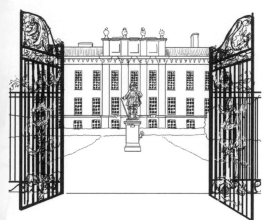

Kensington Palace

WILD BOY PETER

In 1725, a young boy was found living wild in woods near Hanover in Germany.

Peter was brought to London and spent time at the court of King George I, where he became a celebrity. A famous author wrote a book on him, and Peter had his portrait painted along with other members of the court. The painting can still be seen at Kensington Palace today.

Using the grid lines to help you, draw your own version of the Wild Boy Peter in the bigger grid opposite.

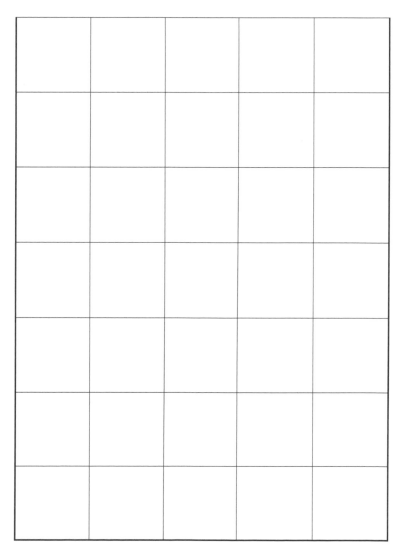

FIRE! FIRE!

In 1666, the Great Fire of London raged through the city. Londoners gathered their most precious belongings and tried to leave town. Race your friends to see who can get out of the city first!

For this game you will need a dice and counters. Start at the bakery on Pudding Lane, where the fire started. The aim is to get to the River Thames where it is safe. Good luck!

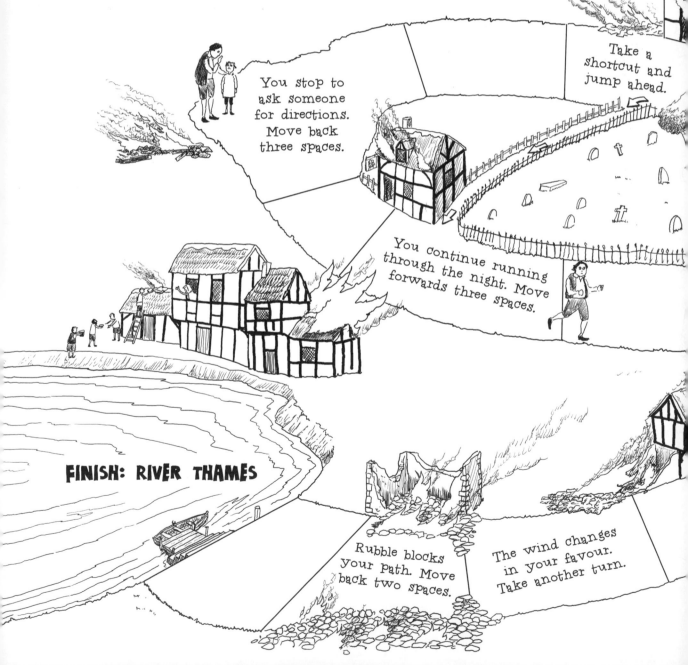

Take a shortcut and jump ahead.

You stop to ask someone for directions. Move back three spaces.

You continue running through the night. Move forwards three spaces.

FINISH: RIVER THAMES

Rubble blocks your path. Move back two spaces.

The wind changes in your favour. Take another turn.

START: PUDDING LANE

DID YOU KNOW?

London's Great Fire started in the early hours of the morning at the house and shop of Thomas Farynor (the king's baker) in Pudding Lane, near London Bridge. Thomas forgot to fully extinguish his baking oven and by the afternoon the smoke from the fire could be seen as far away as Oxford (96 km/60 miles away!).

You stop to bury your favourite teddy bear to save him from the fire. Miss a turn.

You scurry through a tunnel. Jump ahead.

A friend gives you a lift on their cart. Roll again to take another turn.

You stop to help people who are using hooks to pull down flammable buildings. Miss a go.

You stop to help throw water on the fire. Miss a turn.

COLOUR IN THE MONUMENT TO THE GREAT FIRE.

COLOUR IN ST PAUL'S CATHEDRAL.

COLOUR IN THIS
TRAFFIC JAM.

DID YOU KNOW?
Miniatures were mini portraits of people and they were popular in the Elizabethan period. Many of Queen Elizabeth I's subjects wore a miniature of her as a way of showing their admiration.

Draw some miniature masterpieces.

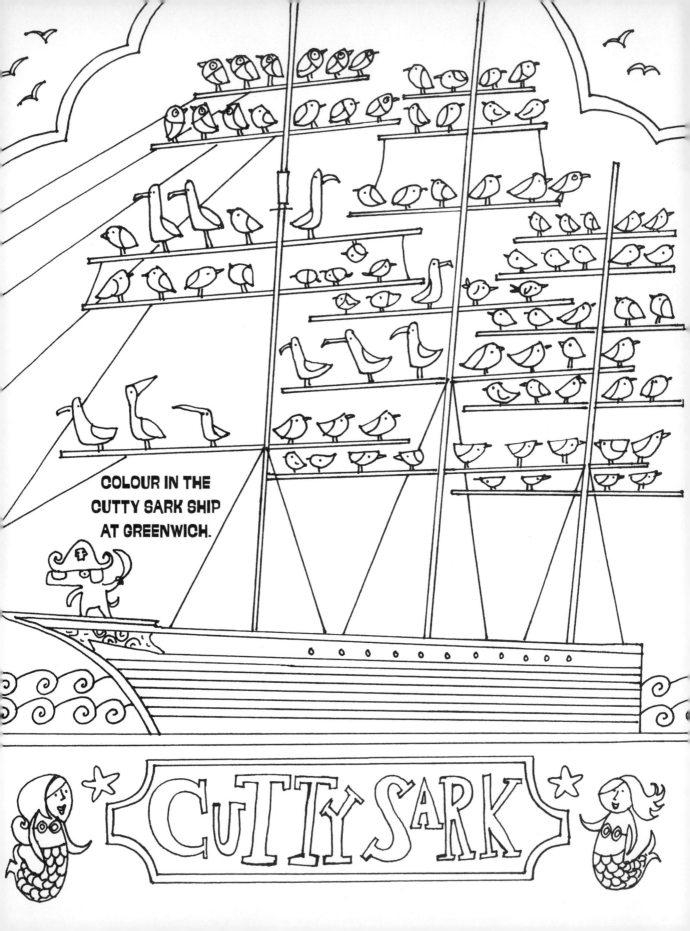

COLOUR IN THE
CUTTY SARK SHIP
AT GREENWICH.

CUTTY SARK

WHERE IN THE WORLD?

For centuries, all kinds of goods have been brought to Britain on huge ships from other countries around the world.

Use this map to work out where each of these items were brought from during the reign of Queen Elizabeth I. To find out which country the items came from you will need to use co-ordinates. A co-ordinate is a letter and a number that refers to a location on a map. To use a co-ordinate, place your finger on the number on the left-hand side of the map. Trace your finger along the row to the column that matches the letter. In that square you will find the country that the item is from. The answers are on page 64.

1. Silk (H3)
2. Spices (G3)
3. Furs (G2)
4. Carpets (F3)
5. Oranges (E3)

EXTRA CHALLENGE

Can you find the co-ordinates for:
• A whale   • A polar bear
• A mermaid

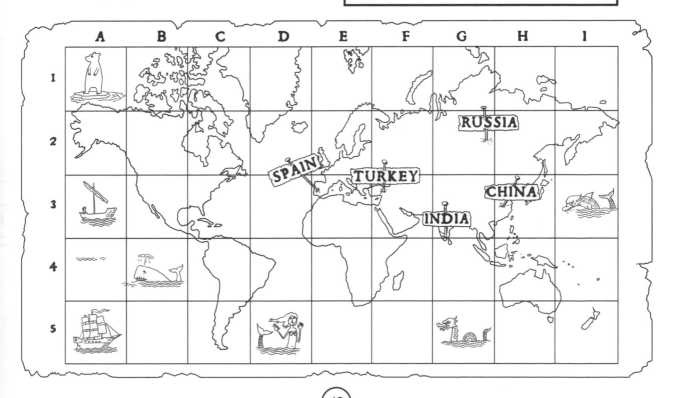

COLOUR IN KEW GARDENS
WITH FLOWER POWER.

45

KEW PALACE
SPOT THE DIFFERENCE

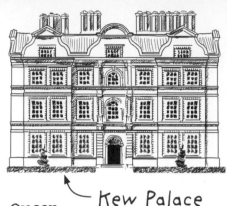

Kew Palace

Kew Palace was home to King George III, Queen Charlotte and some of their 15 children.

The royal kids are causing all kinds of mischief. Can you spot 10 differences between the pictures below? Check the answers on page **64**.

COLOUR IN
WESTMINSTER ABBEY.

GRUESOME GHOSTS

It is said that London's palaces are filled with gruesome ghosts who haunt the buildings. Spook yourself with these scary stories.

HAUNTED GALLERY

Legend has it that the ghost of Catherine Howard haunts a gallery at Hampton Court. Catherine, the fifth wife of King Henry VIII, was dragged kicking and screaming through the gallery by guards who had arrested her for having other boyfriends. Inexplicably, people often feel strange and even faint at very specific points in the gallery today. Would you dare go there?

CAUGHT ON CAMERA

At Hampton Court, a ghostly figure, known as 'skeletor', was caught on CCTV. Doors mysteriously flew open on three different days and staff and visitors reported seeing a ghostly figure.

GRIZZLY GHOST

In 1811, George III was given a grizzly bear and he kept it at the Tower of London. The ghost of the bear is said to haunt the Tower, and once appeared to a guard who was so frightened that it is said he died on the spot.

THE GREY LADY

The ghost of the royal servant Dame Sybil Penn, also known as the 'Grey Lady', is said to haunt Hampton Court. The tomb where the Grey Lady was buried was moved when a nearby church was rebuilt, and soon after strange noises and ghostly apparitions began to appear. One time, the sound of a person working at a spinning wheel was heard through a wall. Members of staff followed the noise and found a room that they hadn't known existed ... it contained a spinning wheel!

COLOUR IN THIS WILD WESTMINSTER SCENE.

MAKE YOUR OWN BUCKINGHAM PALACE GUARD

They're changing guards at Buckingham Palace! This is when one regiment guarding the King and his London palaces is replaced by a new one.

The guards' uniform is very smart. They wear a red coat, black trousers and a tall black hat. Join in the fun by making your very own guard.

YOU WILL NEED:
- A cardboard tube
- 2 sheets of A4 paper
- A pencil
- Scissors
- Coloured paints or pens
- Glue or sticky tape.

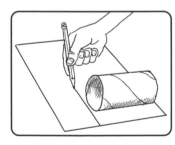

1. Place the cardboard tube so that the bottom of it lines up with the bottom of one of the pieces of paper.

2. Use the pencil to mark where the top of the tube comes up to. Fold the piece of paper at this point and cut along the fold.

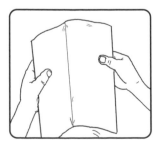

3. Take the piece of paper that is now the same length as the cardboard tube and fold it in half horizontally, then open it back up again.

4. Paint or colour the section of paper above the fold red and the section below the fold black.

5. On the second piece of paper, trace over each of the shapes on the opposite page and use the paints or pens to colour them in. Leave them to dry.

6. When the black and red piece of paper is dry, wrap it around the cardboard tube and stick in place. The top half will become the guard's jacket and the bottom half will become his trousers.

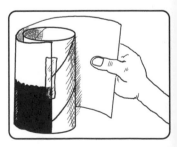

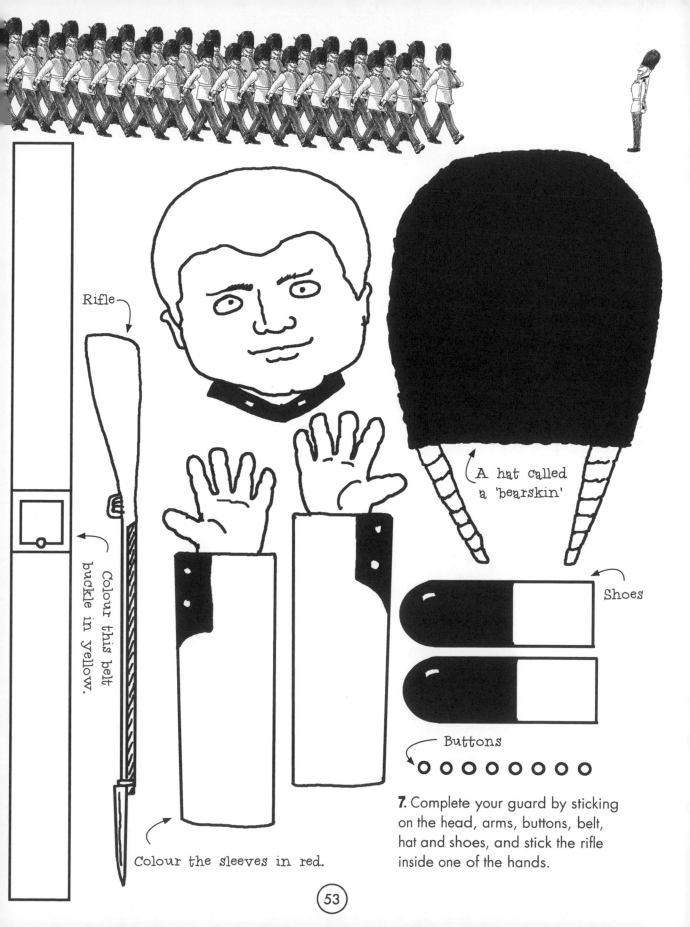

Rifle

Colour this belt
buckle in yellow.

Colour the sleeves in red.

A hat called
a 'bearskin'

Shoes

Buttons

7. Complete your guard by sticking
on the head, arms, buttons, belt,
hat and shoes, and stick the rifle
inside one of the hands.

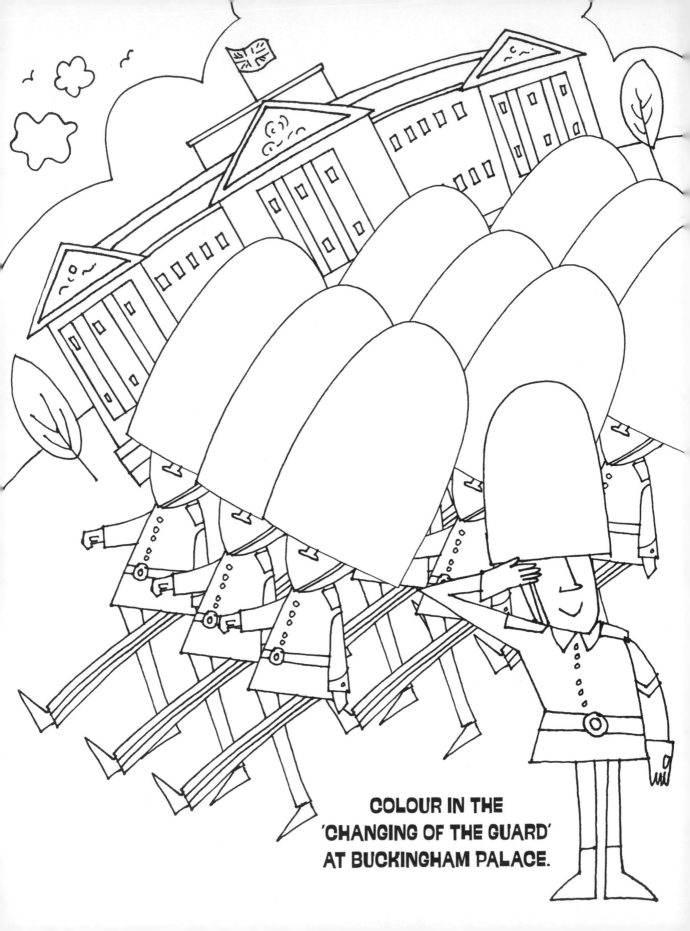

COLOUR IN THE 'CHANGING OF THE GUARD' AT BUCKINGHAM PALACE.

THE BANQUETING HOUSE

The Banqueting House in Whitehall was designed for King James I as a grand venue for royal receptions, ceremonies and the performance of 'masques' (entertainment that included singing and dancing).

The building is perhaps most famous for being the site where Charles I was executed. Charles was defeated in the English Civil War (between the Royalists, who were supporters of the King, and the Parliamentarians who fought againt him). He was put on trial and sentenced to death 'by the severing of his head from his body'.

On 30th January 1649, Charles I was led to a scaffold that had been especially erected outside the Banqueting House. It is said that he met his death with great courage and dignity.

DID YOU KNOW?

Charles was executed on a freezing cold day that would have made anyone shiver, but he didn't want anyone to think that he was shaking from fear, so he wore two shirts!

You are invited by the court of James I to a Masque, on Twelfth night 1622

Guests can wear fancy dress costumes of their choice to attend this event hosted by the King. Design fun and fancy outfits to wear to the masque.

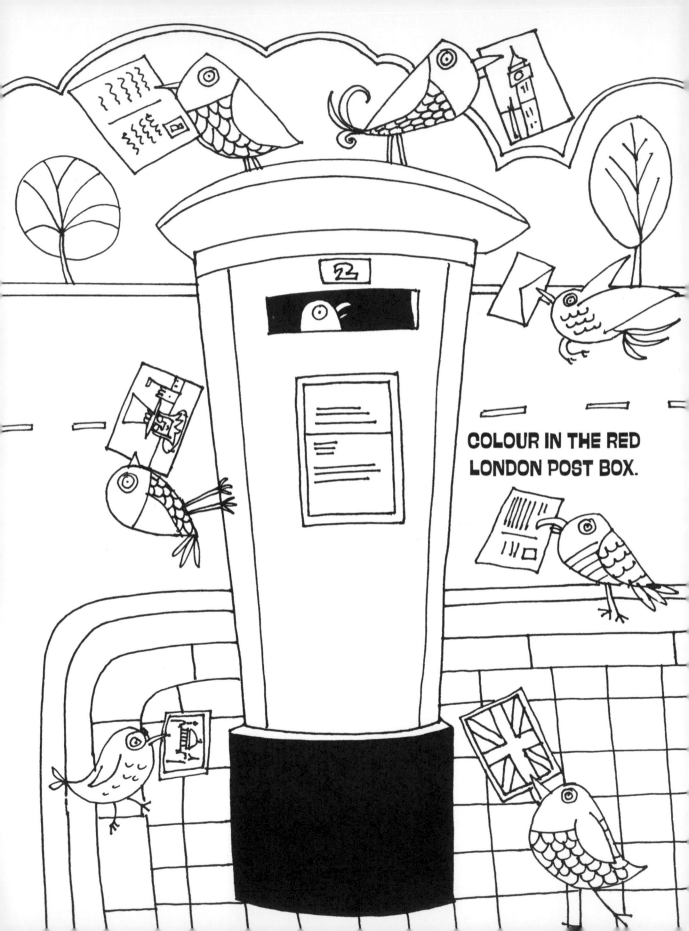

COLOUR IN THE RED LONDON POST BOX.

DID YOU KNOW?

In the sixteenth century, fashion was a way of showing off your wealth. The more extravagant the dresses and accessories, the richer the person. Elizabeth I was thought to own 300 fancy gowns!

Decorate her dress.

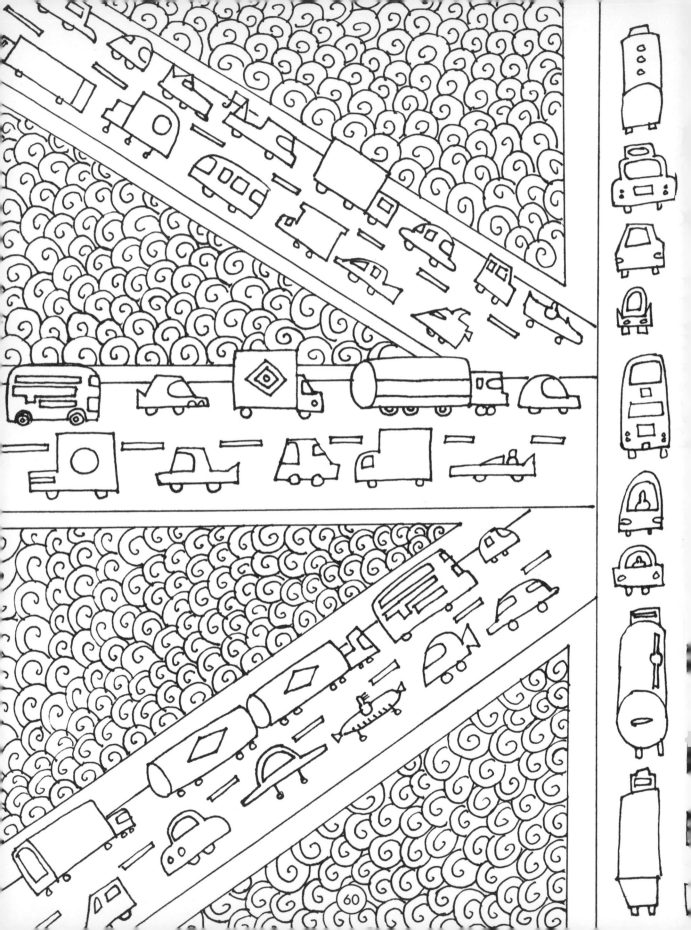

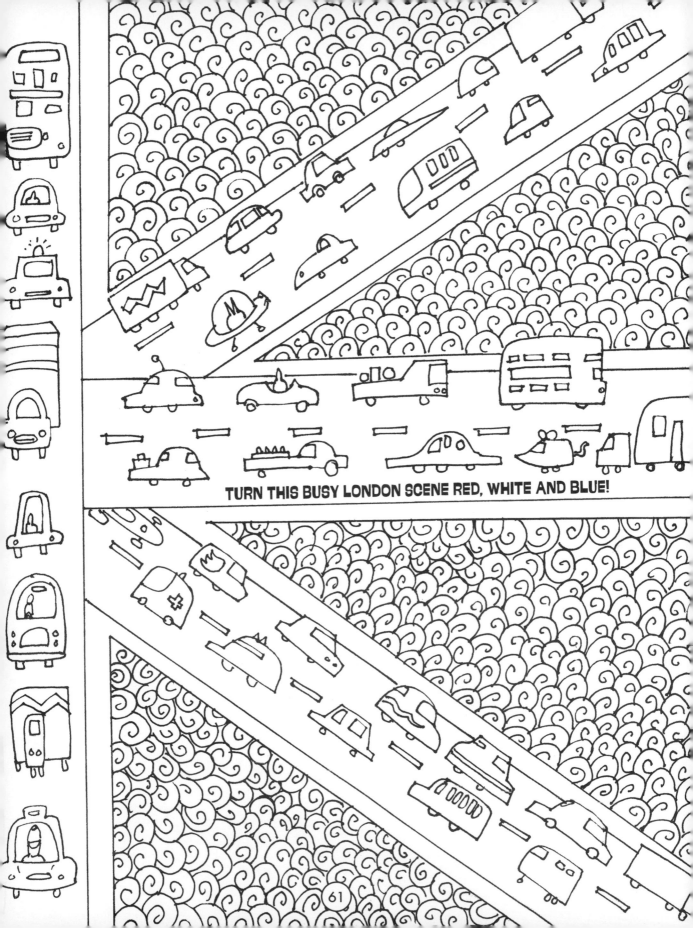

TURN THIS BUSY LONDON SCENE RED, WHITE AND BLUE!

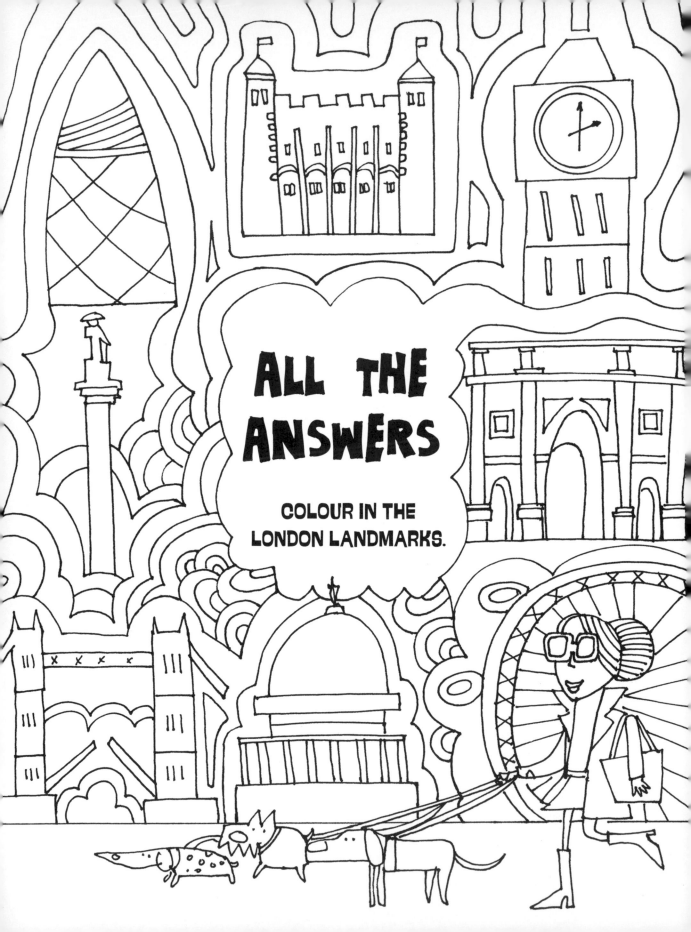

ALL THE ANSWERS

COLOUR IN THE LONDON LANDMARKS.

THE TOWER OF LONDON
PAGES 6 AND 7

MOAT GETAWAY:
The prisoner carries the Yeoman Warder across the moat, leaves him on the other side, and comes back. The prisoner then carries the lion across, picks up the Yeoman Warder, and takes him back to the Tower-side of the moat. The prisoner picks up the jewels and takes them over to the other side, where the lion is waiting. Finally, he goes back across the moat to pick up the Yeoman Warder and take him back over to the other side.

THE ROYAL MENAGERIE:

A lion had its own specially built tower in the grounds.

A zebra drank ale from the soldiers' canteen.

A leopard tore up visitors' umbrellas.

An ostrich was fed nails as people believed it could digest metal.

A polar bear fished in the River Thames.

ARRANGE THE ARMOURY:

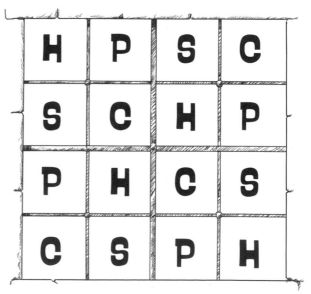

H	P	S	C
S	C	H	P
P	H	C	S
C	S	P	H

RAVENS:
There are 7 ravens hiding across pages 6 and 7 … did you spot them all?
Page 6: on the tower at the top of the page; flying above the 'Moat Getaway' title; hiding in the boat; standing to the right of the Yeoman Warder.
Page 7: two in the top right corner; behind the scroll.

SAVE THE CROWN JEWELS!
PAGE 13

THE CARDINAL SPIDER WEB
PAGE 27

Spider A frightened Henry VIII.
Spider B frightened Anne Boleyn.
Spider C frightened Thomas Wolsey.
Spider D frightened the cook.

WHERE IN THE WORLD?
PAGE 43

1. China
2. India
3. Russia
4. Turkey
5. Spain

Extra challenge:
Whale (B4)
Polar bear (A1)
Mermaid (D5)

THE GRUESOME AILMENTS OF HENRY VIII
PAGE 17

1. D	3. A	5. C
2. B	4. E	

KEW PALACE SPOT THE DIFFERENCE
PAGE 46

AMAZING MAZE
PAGE 23